Weather Wise

Rain

Helen Cox Cannons

Raintree is an imprint of Capstone Global Library Limited,
a company incorporated in England and Wales having
its registered office at 7 Pilgrim Street, London, EC4V 6LB –
Registered company number: 6695582

www.raintreepublishers.co.uk
myorders@raintreepublishers.co.uk

Edited by Siân Smith and John-Paul Wilkins
Designed by Philippa Jenkins
Picture research by Ruth Blair
Production by Victoria Fitzgerald
Originated by Capstone Global Library Ltd
Printed and bound in China

ISBN 978 1 4062 8478 2
18 17 16 15 14
10 9 8 7 6 5 4 3 2 1

British Library Cataloguing in Publication Data
A full catalogue record for this book is available from the
British Library.

Acknowledgements
We would like to thank the following for permission to reproduce
photographs: Corbis: Steve Cole/Anyone/amanaimages,
cover; Dreamstime: Egonzitter, 22, Hassanmohiudin, 4, Qwasyx,
18; iStockphoto: aimintang, 14, 23 (bottom), IsaacLKoval, 6,
23 (top), Krakozawr, 5, oriba, 20; Shutterstock: Balazs Kovacs,
21, Charlie Edward, 11, 23 (second from bottom), Dirk Ott, 10,
Huansheng Xu, 7, leospek, 9, Matej Hudovernik, 8, 23 (middle),
Viorel Sima, 15; SuperStock: Lisette Le Bon, 19

We would like to thank John Horel for his invaluable help in the
preparation of this book.

Every effort has been made to contact copyright holders of
material reproduced in this book. Any omissions will be rectified
in subsequent printings if notice is given to the publisher.

Contents

What is rain?. 4

Types of rain 6

How does rain form? 12

What do you wear in
    rainy weather? 18

How does rain help us? 20

Did you know? 22

Picture glossary 23

Index 24

Notes for parents and teachers 24

What is rain?

Rain is water that falls from clouds.

Rain feels wet on your skin.

Types of rain

When rain falls, it can be light rain.

This is sometimes called **drizzle**.

When rain falls, it can be heavy rain.
This is sometimes called a downpour.

In some places, it does not rain for a long time. There is not enough water.

This is called a **drought**.

In some places, it rains for a long
time. There is too much water.

This is called a **flood**.

How does rain form?

One raindrop is made from tiny drops of water. Each tiny drop is called a **droplet**.

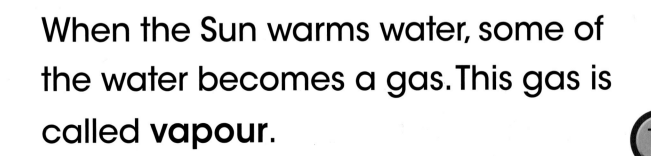

When the Sun warms water, some of the water becomes a gas. This gas is called **vapour**.

Vapour comes from oceans, rivers and lakes. Vapour even comes from puddles.

Vapour also comes from plants
and animals. We usually cannot
see this vapour.

The vapour rises into the air. Then it cools down and turns into droplets. The droplets make clouds.

The droplets join together and form raindrops. When the raindrops get too heavy, they fall to the ground.

What do you wear in rainy weather?

When it rains, you could wear a raincoat.

When it rains, you could also
use an umbrella.

How does rain help us?

Rain brings water back down to Earth. It keeps the oceans filled.

Rain helps plants grow.

Did you know?

Forests that have a lot of rain are called rainforests.

Picture glossary

drizzle light rain

droplet tiny
drop of water

drought long period
without rainfall

flood large amount of water
that spreads over dry land

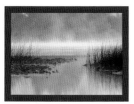

vapour gas created by
heating water

Index

animal 15

cloud 4, 16

droplet 12 ,16, 17, 23

plant 15, 21

vapour 13, 14, 15, 16, 23

Notes for parents and teachers

Before reading

Assess background knowledge. Ask: What is rain? How does rain form? How does rain help us?

After reading

Recall and reflection: Ask children if their ideas about rain at the beginning were correct. What new facts about rain did they learn?

Sentence knowledge: Ask children to look at page 13. How many sentences are on the page? Ask them to point to the beginning and end of one sentence.

Word recognition: Ask children to point at the word *some* on pages 8 and 10. Can they think of another word that means about the same as *some*?